A WOMAN'S BIRTHDAY WISH

Written and Illustrated By:
Jerry King

30 29 28 27 26 25 24 23 22 21 20 19 18 17 16 15 14 13 12 11 10 9 8 7 6 5 4 3 2 1

Ivory Tower Publishing Co., Inc.
125 Walnut St., P.O. Box 9132, Watertown, MA 02272-9132
Telephone #: (617) 923-1111   Fax #: (617) 923-8839

Female nudity would be banned from movies, while nudity of leading men would be common practice.

Men would have to wear their hair long and spend countless hours and an outrageous amount of money in beauty salons to satisfy society's standards. However, it would be acceptable for a woman to simply throw on a hat when going out.

Men would have periods and all that accompany them such as: cramps, mood swings and water retention.

Romance would not be an outdated concept.
Men would no longer define a date as a six-pack of beer,
a sports bloopers video and a quick hop in the sack.

The amount of beer and junk food consumed by men would be greatly limited, thus, eliminating unsightly beer bellies.

Men would like to get dressed up. This would eliminate hours of moaning about how much they hate wearing a tie.

Men would have enough sense to hire a professional when they themselves are too proud to admit they are unable to do the job.

Men would have more to talk about than sex.

Men would be responsible for bearing children. With this responsibility would come weight gain, stretch marks and the ever popular morning sickness.

Men would take the same pride in the appearance of the house as they do in their car, tools and golf clubs.

Certain men would wear pants that fit, thus,
eliminating unsightly butt cracks.

All macho-type movies in video stores would be replaced
by such classics as "Gone With The Wind" and "My Fair Lady."

Men would get their own life instead of living
vicariously through various sports personalities.

Jobs like mowing the lawn, taking out the trash
and fixing the sink would actually get done.

Men would admit when they're lost.

Men who snore would be required to have corrective surgery.

Men in high ranking executive positions would be replaced by women. Men would still be required to do the same amount of work but for only half the pay.

Cupid's arrow would find much better targets.

Men would no longer define a night on the town
as a quick burger and a Sylvester Stallone video.

To fully appreciate what it feels like to be hot and have backaches, men would have breasts and wear bras.

Anything that falls under the category of work
would be considered "Man's" work.

Men wouldn't feel the need to prove they're macho
by cheating or flirting with other women.

Any man found guilty of sexual harassment would
be subject to a stiff fine and/or hard labor.

Grocery shopping would be the man's responsibility. <u>However</u>, only nutritious items would be bought.

Being a housewife would be a $100,000 a year job.

Men would be harassed, exploited and degraded sexually.

Men would no longer act as if their very lives
depended on the win or loss of a sports team.

Men would love wearing a tie and jacket.

Men would actually call a woman after asking for her phone number.

Men must regularly attend classes that teach "NO MEANS NO."

Men would always have the burden of feeling inadequate unless they weighed 110 pounds, had perfect hair and a perfect complexion.

Murder would be against the law. However, it would be legal to shoot a man in a leisure suit who uses such lines as, "What's your sign?", "Hey, Babe, like my new gold chain?" or "Do you come here often?"

Men would not only be responsible for holding down a full-time job, but would then come home to resume their duties as house-cleaner and cook.

Men would be required to shave 90% of their bodies. Areas in which unwanted hair is most prevalent would be subject to waxing or plucking.

Men would be required to wear items of uncomfortable clothing such as bras, girdles and high heels.

Sitting on a toilet in which the seat had been carelessly left up would not be a concern because all toilets would come with lids in the permanent down position, thus, leaving men to sit for all occasions.

Soap operas would replace sports on Sundays.

Men would have to endure rude sexual comments
delivered by obnoxious construction persons.

Obnoxious sounds, gestures or mannerisms would be illegal.
If found guilty of scratching, farting, burping or any other facet of
being a pig, one could face a stiff fine or, in extreme cases, jail time.

Men would fix things in a timely and prompt manner.

Men wouldn't be so competitive over the most meaningless things.

Birth control would be the man's responsibility.

Men's popularity would be based on their sensitivity and tastefulness rather than how much beer they could swill.

Men who ignore ecologically responsible attitudes would
be assigned living quarters near toxic waste dumps.

Men wouldn't try to match their high school performances.

Men would generate their greatest enthusiasm
for home and yard activities.

Snuggling and after-play would last more than 8 seconds.

Men would not consider romance a bottle
of cheap wine and an X-rated movie.

All women's phone calls would be considered reasonable
and necessary interruptions to family life.

All men would be sufficiently skilled at love-making to make it unnecessary for women to pretend.

Luxurious bathrooms with personal attendants
would be considered a budget necessity.

Men wouldn't have this overwhelming desire
to impose their hobbies on you.

Men would love to shop and insist upon continuing until closing time.

Men would love to take home economics courses that concentrate on gourmet cooking.

Divorce settlements would be equitable
with each party getting what they deserve.

Men would have the confidence and imagination to plan an evening.

Men's fantasies would change from sexual perversions
to love and romantic situations.

There would never be any doubt on what to wear because men would always take a woman somewhere classy.

Women on TV, in the movies and in magazines
would be at least five pounds overweight.

Comfort would take a back-seat to style and taste
when men dressed for a date.

Football, basketball, hockey and baseball would all fall in the same one-month season.

Men would develop a neatness compulsion that would kick in whenever the sink filled with dishes.

Men would join family get-togethers rather
than hibernate in front of the TV.

Men would recognize the wisdom of investing
in fine jewelry for a woman.

All men would come with a gene that makes them
subservient to women.

A penis and hormones would be given out on a trial basis only.
Those who didn't act responsibly would have to forfeit them.

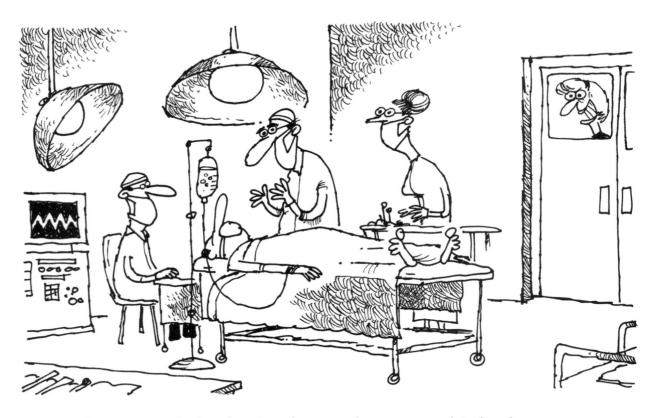

The part of the brain that makes men think about sex
all the time could be surgically removed.

Bachelor parties would be planned by the bride.
Poetry readers would replace strippers.

Men would always remember special occasions
such as anniversaries and birthdays.

Gymnastics and figure skating would be given
equal time with football and basketball.

Remote controls would come with a device that delivers
a small electrical charge to any adult male hand.

Women would fit into their wedding dress forever.

A book containing the answers to why men do the things they do would be available at libraries and book stores.

Women would be treated with the same respect that men give their car.

Men would have the honor of receiving a yearly pelvic exam. To make each visit a memorable one, all instruments would be stored in the freezer.

Women would be able to indulge all their food cravings while men would have to watch everything they ate.

Flowers would be an instinctive cultural gift that men would buy as easily as a 6-pack of beer.

Men wouldn't go through a metamorphoses following the honeymoon.

Men would love romantic entertainment.

Men would tell the truth, no matter how incriminating.

Women could leave work early to take care of
"important matters" while men "hold the fort."

Every woman administrator would receive recognition
and honors at least once a month.

Men would get sweet cravings at "that time of the month."

Men would not feel that asking directions was
an infringement on their manliness.

Banks would acknowledge women as much better credit risks.

Men would assume the responsibility of changing diapers and feeding the baby in the wee hours of the morning.

Men would become emotional on anniversaries and special occasions.

Men wouldn't assume women always wanted company.

Men would ask women for help and advice when shopping for cars.

Men would always check with the woman before buying clothes.